This book is a work of nonfiction based on the
author's personal experiences. Certain names,
locations, and identifying details have been
changed to protect the privacy of individuals.

Self Published by: Stitched Intentions Press
Elizabeth, NJ via Bronx, NY

ISBN: 9798308379836

Printed in the United States of America

First Edition
2025

For information, permissions, or inquiries,
contact: Jacqueline Rodriguez-Falla
@Stitchedtogetherwgintentions

Dedication

To My Best Friend, My Husband. Thank you for showing me what true love looks like. Your unwavering support, patience, and kindness have been my greatest blessings. You have loved me through every chapter of my story, and with you, I've found a love that feels whole and safe. You inspire me every day to be the best version of myself, and I'm forever grateful to walk through life by your side. I love you.

To My Children and Grandchildren, You are my heart, my strength, and my reason for everything. Each of you has brought an indescribable joy and love into my life. You've taught me what resilience, hope, and unconditional love truly means. This book is for you— for the lessons we've learned together, the love we've shared, and the legacy I hope to leave behind.

TABLE OF
CONTENTS

Prologue: A Life Changing Moment

I sat on the edge of the bed, staring at the crib across the room as if my entire existence hinged on the small, rhythmic rise and fall of her tiny chest. The night was still, but inside me, everything was crumbling. My body ached—not just from the bruises he left on my skin, but from the weight I carried in my heart. It wasn't the kind of pain anyone could see. It lived in the silence, in the isolation, in the words that replayed over and over in my head: You're nothing without me.

That night, everything felt too heavy.
Too loud. Too hopeless.

I didn't recognize myself anymore. I was exhausted—physically, mentally, spiritually. I was tired of pretending, tired of making excuses, tired of hiding the scars, tired of feeling like I didn't matter. The woman I used to be—the dreamer, the mother, the fighter—had disappeared beneath years of manipulation and fear.

Prologue: A Life Changing Moment

The house was quiet, but my mind wasn't. His words echoed in my head like a broken record, reminding me that I was worthless, reminding me that no one would love me, reminding me that I had no way out.

I looked at my daughter.

She was so small, so innocent, so unaware of the storm that raged around her. Her little hands were curled near her face, her breath soft and steady. She didn't know how much she saved me every single day without even trying.

And yet, in that moment, I almost gave up.

The darkness whispered to me, convincing me that it would be easier if I just stopped fighting. Easier if I gave in, if I disappeared. I thought about how tired I was. I thought about how I didn't want to hurt anymore. I thought about how maybe everyone would be better off without me.

Prologue: A Life Changing Moment

But then... I thought about her.

If I left, he would win. If I left, she would stay in the chaos I couldn't bear anymore. If I left, she would suffer in ways I knew too well. And she deserved more. She deserved peace. She deserved love. She deserved a mother who would fight for her, even when she had nothing left to give.

So I sat there on the edge of the bed and I made a promise—to her, to myself, to the woman I used to be and the woman I hoped to become again.

I promised that I wouldn't give up.

I didn't know how I was going to leave. I didn't know how I was going to survive. But I knew I had to try. For her. For me. For the life we both deserved.

Prologue: A Life Changing Moment

That night changed everything. It was the moment I realized that I couldn't keep living in survival mode. I had to find a way out. I had to find my way back to myself.

And while I didn't know it then, that decision—the choice to stay alive, to fight—would eventually lead me to something beautiful. It would lead me to freedom. It would lead me to healing. And one day, it would lead me to love.

Before The Storm

Before the chaos, before the pain, before the nights I spent crying myself to sleep—I was just me.

Hi, I'm Jacqueline. I am an only child, and I was born and raised in the Bronx to two dreamers from Puerto Rico who came to New York in search of opportunity and a better life. My parents arrived with hopes of building something meaningful, but life didn't turn out the way they had planned. When I was 5 years old, their relationship ended, and my father moved out of our lives. I didn't understand it then, but it was the beginning of a new chapter for my mother, my grandmother, and me. My grandfather and My uncle were also in the household. But, those are other chapters in my life that one day I will elaborate on.

My father passed away when I was 10, his life cut short by cardiac arrest due to liver cirrhosis and alcoholism.. His loss left a void in my life, but it also left me with lessons about resilience and strength—lessons I would only come to understand years later.

I was raised by three incredible women, my grandmother. my mother, and my aunt who became my pillars of strength. They taught me how to stand on my own, how to be independent, and how to find joy even in the hardest of times.

Our home was always filled with music, from the rhythms of salsa and merengue to soulful ballads. Music became a constant in my life, a source of comfort and expression. Til' this day, if there's music playing, I'm singing. And if there's a dance floor, I'm the first one on it. So, now you know how I've been able to deal with my trauma. Music heals my soul each and every day.

When I became pregnant at the age of 17. I didn't imagine being a single mother at the mere age of 18. Some might have thought my hopes and dreams ended there. But the truth is that's when they began. My Son became my motivation, my reason for striving for something more. With the support of my mother, who helped me raise my three children so I could work and attend school, I kept moving forward.

I didn't finish my college degree back then. Life had other plans for me. But here I am now, on the brink of graduating with my associate's degree, with my eyes set on a bachelor's and maybe even a master's. Every step I've taken, every challenge I've faced, has led me to this moment.

I was a woman with dreams, a mother with hope, and a daughter carrying forward the lessons of three strong women. And while life would test me in unimaginable ways, those roots of strength and love would carry me through.

CHAPTER 1

The Storm In Disguise

It started on a warm summer day at the Bronx Criminal Court. Jury duty wasn't where anyone expected to find a new chapter of their life, but that's where I met him. I didn't notice him at first—just another face in a room full of strangers waiting for the hours to pass. On the third day, as we were being dismissed, he walked over, his smile easy, his demeanor warm.

We talked briefly, and before we left, he handed me his phone number. "If you ever want to hang out," he said, "give me a call."

Looking back now, I wonder how many other women have stories that start this way. How many of us met our storms wrapped in charm, thinking we had found something good? If someone had told me that day that the man smiling at me across the jury room would become my greatest nightmare, I would've laughed. It's strange how hindsight feels like a warning you never heard.

In the weeks after jury duty, when I finally decided to call him, I remember feeling nervous but excited. As a young mother, I didn't get many chances to feel seen outside of motherhood and work. He made me feel like a woman again —not just a mom, not just someone struggling to make ends meet, but someone worthy of attention.

Our first date was simple. We grabbed coffee and walked around, talking about life, about our childhoods in New York, He asked questions about me, seemed genuinely interested in my story. It felt nice—refreshing even. No one had asked about me in a long time without expecting something in return.

I told myself it was fate. Maybe this was how new beginnings started.

He started calling regularly, and every time the phone rang, my heart skipped. He was attentive, funny, and sweet. We spoke every morning. Always telling me to have a good day. He showed up with flowers just because. He took me to restaurants I'd never been to, introducing me to new foods, new experiences.

And slowly, I started to trust him.

I had no reason not to. I was young, single, trying to balance motherhood and work. He seemed kind, charming even. So, whenever he invited me out, I said yes.

I had no idea then that I wasn't walking into a relationship—I was walking into a storm that would almost destroy me.

It didn't happen overnight. Abuse rarely does. It creeps in slowly, hiding behind smiles, apologies, and small, subtle cuts you convince yourself aren't really wounds.

But there were little things—small moments—that made my stomach twist, even if I couldn't explain why at the time.

The first time he commented on how I dressed, it didn't seem like much. "You're so beautiful, baby," he'd say, "but you don't need to wear clothes like that. You should look more elegant."

It sounded like a compliment, wrapped in care, so I shrugged it off. But it wasn't care. It was control.

The first time he didn't answer my calls for a whole day because I went out with a friend, he said he was just upset I hadn't included him. "It's not that I don't trust you," he explained, "I just miss you when you're gone."

And I believed him. Because when you want something to be real, you'll convince yourself of anything.

Looking back now, there were so many red flags—so many flashing, screaming signs that I should have walked away—but I ignored every single one of them. I didn't want to see them. I wanted so badly to believe in the good in him, in the future I thought we could build, that I looked the other way every time he showed me exactly who he was.

In the beginning, he was everything I thought I needed. I was a young mother trying to make life work, and here was this man who made me feel seen. He called when he said he would. He opened doors, took me out to restaurants I had never been to, bought me gifts. He made me feel special—something I hadn't felt in a long time.

But almost immediately, the small things started.

And then he started making comments on how I should fix my hair, how I should act. He made me feel like he was just paying attention, like he cared enough to want me to "do better." I convinced myself that was love—someone who wanted the best for me. What I didn't realize was that he was slowly shaping me into who he wanted me to be, chipping away at who I actually was.

One day, early in our relationship, I brought my son with me to meet him. And instead of embracing the idea of my child being part of my life, he looked at me coldly and asked, "Why did you bring him?"

My son, though, saw through him long before I did.

My son was quiet around him, unsure. He would cling to me a little tighter when he was around, watching with careful eyes. He never said much—children know when it's safer to stay silent—but I could see it in his body language. The way he shrank when that man walked into a room. The way he glanced at me for reassurance.

I should have paid more attention.

That should have been the first major red flag. But instead, I made excuses. I told myself maybe he wasn't ready to be around children. I convinced myself it wasn't a big deal.

My son, however, knew the truth long before I did. He began to distance himself, reluctant to be around this man who made his mother tense, quiet, and small. He felt the shift that I kept trying to ignore.

And still, I stayed.

When we moved in together within the first year, the atmosphere in our home shifted almost immediately. He wanted to know where I was at all times. He questioned everything I did, every decision I made. But it was always masked as "concern" or "love."

The house we shared was neat, decorated carefully to make it feel like a home. But it never felt like mine. It felt like a place I was allowed to exist in—as long as I played by his rules.

I recall one day we had what I named as "the bank incident"and this is when things really began to crack, though even then, I told myself it was nothing. One afternoon, the bank called while he wasn't home. They asked if he lived at our address, and without thinking, I said yes. Why wouldn't I? It was the truth.

When he came home and found out, his rage was explosive. He yelled at me like I was a child who had done something unforgivable. "Don't ever answer my calls!" he screamed, his face twisted in fury. I stood there, stunned, unsure how something so small could cause such anger.

And then, without warning, his hands were around my neck.

In that moment, I couldn't breathe. I couldn't move. And when he let go, just as suddenly, he cried. He apologized. He told me he didn't mean it.

That night, I couldn't sleep. I stared at the ceiling, feeling like I was floating above my body. I wanted to leave. I wanted to run. But then I thought about rent, about my son, about how tired I was. I could've went home to my mom. But, didn't want anyone to know what was going on.

I thought about how leaving meant starting over with nothing. That should have been the moment I walked away for good.

I stayed because I wanted to believe it was a one-time thing. I stayed because I wanted to believe in the man he was when he wasn't angry—the man who made me laugh, who took me to dinner, who bought me clothes.

The red flags kept coming. The controlling comments. The accusations. The coldness that appeared out of nowhere. And still, I stayed.

What no one tells you about abuse is that it's not just the physical bruises that break you—it's the silence afterward. It's the way you stop recognizing yourself in the mirror. The way you become small, careful, invisible, just to avoid the next explosion.

He chipped away at me piece by piece.
He made me doubt every decision.
He made me question whether anyone else would want me.

And that's how he kept me there.
Not with force—but with fear and doubt.

There was one night we argued—I can't even remember over what. But this time, I had finally had enough. I told him I wanted to leave.

That's when he calmly, methodically, walked to a drawer and pulled out a gun. He pointed it at me, as casually as if he were pointing a finger.

The air left my body. Everything inside me froze. He didn't have to say anything; the message was clear. "You leave, and this is how it ends."

The calmness in his voice chilled me more than the weapon in his hand. "The only way you're leaving is in a body bag," he said, like it was nothing.

Somehow, I found the strength to grab my son and run.
Somehow, I survived that night.

But I didn't leave for good. Because the cycle doesn't end when you run—it ends when you finally believe you deserve better. And back then, I wasn't there yet

He called. He apologized. He cried. He promised. He said he couldn't live without me. That he would change. That he needed me.

And I wanted so badly to believe him.

Because believing meant I didn't have to start over.
Believing meant I didn't have to face the terrifying question:
How do I leave? But deep down, I knew.
The storm wasn't outside of me anymore—it was inside me.
And it was only going to get worse.

I knew I shouldn't have. But, I returned to the apartment. I was still numb, unsure of what I'd find. And what I saw broke me in a whole new way. When I walked through the door, the silence was thick—but what I saw next took my breath away for an entirely different reason. Every single item of clothing he had ever bought me was destroyed.

Slashed. Torn. Shredded into pieces. As if my belongings were the enemy. He knew how much I had loved those gifts—especially My Qipao dress I had wanted for so long. Deep red silk with gold embroidery. I had never asked for it, but he knew I wanted it. And when he brought it home, part of me had wanted to believe that maybe, just maybe, he was trying.

But now, it was in ruins. It was more than just clothing on the floor—it was a message. A cruel reminder that anything he gave, he could just as easily take away. That his kindness always came with conditions. That the moment I made him feel powerless, he would strip me of anything that gave me joy. It was a level of emotional violence that spoke louder than words ever could.

That day confirmed what I had tried so hard to ignore: this wasn't love. It was control wrapped in charm. Threats dressed as gifts. A cycle that broke me down piece by piece.

And somewhere inside, I knew—I couldn't keep living like this.

Reflection

If I could go back to the woman I was at the start of this story —the one who met her storm in disguise—I would hold her face in my hands and tell her, "You are enough."

I would tell her that love isn't supposed to make you smaller. That real love doesn't come with conditions, control, or bruises disguised as affection.

I didn't see it then. I wanted so badly to believe in the fairytale that I ignored every red flag. I let myself believe that his smiles and sweet words outweighed the fear and the silence that followed.

But now I know that love should never make you question your worth.

If you're reading this and seeing yourself in these pages, I want you to know—it's not your fault.

You are worthy of a love that feels like peace, not survival.

CHAPTER 2

The Unraveling

Things were going perfect. It finally seemed like everything was falling into place and I thought we were in a loving, and healthy relationship. My son even warmed up to him and he wanted to be part of all the adventures of us.

For a little while, I allowed myself to believe the fairytale. I wanted to believe in the family we were building, in the smiles and the promises and the peaceful days. I convinced myself that the past arguments, the choking incident, the fear I had once felt were all behind us. That maybe, just maybe, this was our new beginning.

We would spend weekends out as a family, taking my son to the park or having dinner together like everything was normal. And there were moments—small, precious moments —when I almost believed it was.

But beneath the smiles, there was still an uneasiness inside me. A voice I kept pushing down that whispered, "Be careful." And then I found out I was pregnant.

When I saw those two pink lines, my heart raced—not just with fear, but with hope. I thought a baby would fix things, that maybe this would finally be enough to make him love me the way I needed to be loved.

In my mind, I was like I'm pregnant. Pregnancy changes everything—or at least, that's what I told myself. I thought that maybe, just maybe, this would soften him. That becoming a father would bring out the best in him. That we would finally become the family I had dreamed of.

For a brief moment, it almost seemed that way. He talked about the baby. He promised to do better. He said we would start fresh.

I imagined a life where he'd step up, where we'd raise our children together in peace.

But that's not how abuse works. It doesn't soften with responsibility. It festers. It grows. My pregnancy didn't change him. It only made him more possessive, more controlling, more dangerous.

The arguments continued, the yelling intensified, and the criticism never stopped. Every day felt like I was walking on eggshells, trying not to set him off. But it never mattered how careful I was—he always found a reason to break me down.

It wasn't just what he said—it was how he said it. The looks. The silence. The way he made me question everything I said, everything I did.

I didn't recognize the woman I had become when I looked in the mirror anymore.

It felt like being trapped in a maze where every turn led to another dead end.

There were days I could barely eat. Nights I laid awake staring at the ceiling, wondering how I ended up here.

And every time I thought about leaving, I reminded myself I was pregnant. That I needed him. That I couldn't do it alone.

And then came the cruise.

Another one of his grand gestures, disguised as an apology. He booked us a vacation—a seven-day cruise, a chance to relax before the baby came. I wanted so badly to believe this was his way of trying, that things were finally going to be different.

But on the second day of the trip, everything unraveled.

It started over something so small—what I ordered for dinner. It sounds ridiculous now, but that's how it always began. He was upset that I hadn't ordered what he wanted. He accused me of being disrespectful, of not considering him.

And just like that, he broke up with me—on a ship in the middle of the ocean. That night in the cabin, I curled up in the bed while he slept soundly beside me, as if he hadn't shattered me hours earlier.

I stared at the ceiling, rocking slightly with the motion of the waves, and wondered how I got here. Alone, pregnant, and trapped—not just on a ship but in a life that felt impossible to escape.

I remember wondering if anyone else on that ship could hear my silent cries. I felt invisible. Powerless. And worse, I felt ashamed that I had allowed it to get this far.

The rest of that trip was a nightmare. He spent every moment ignoring me, belittling me, reminding me that I wasn't good enough. I was trapped on that ship, surrounded by strangers, unable to escape his cruelty. I cried in our cabin every night, wishing I could go home, wishing I could disappear. But the worst was still to come.

A few months later, when I was seven months pregnant, he booked another trip—a vacation to St. Thomas. Another "peace offering," another manipulation wrapped in a gift.
I should have said no. I should have known better. But I went. He always knew how to pull me back in.

It wasn't the gifts—it was the illusion.
He would paint this picture of who he could be: generous, charming, apologetic. And every time I started to build up the courage to leave, he'd dangle a fantasy in front of me—a cruise, a trip, a promise.

And like so many times before, I took the bait.

At first, everything seemed fine. The island was beautiful, the resort luxurious. But paradise means nothing when you carry hell inside you. One night, he got upset again. Over something trivial. I can't even remember what. But I remember how it ended.

He kicked me in the stomach.

Seven months pregnant, and he kicked me so hard I doubled over, terrified for my baby, terrified for myself. I felt the contractions start almost immediately.

It's hard to describe the fear that settles into your bones when you feel your baby react to violence before they've even entered the world.

An ambulance rushed me to the hospital. The doctors worked quickly to stop the labor. I lay there in that hospital bed, praying my daughter would hold on. Praying that she would survive.

And somehow, she did.

Lying in that hospital bed, hearing the monitors beep, watching the nurses rush around me, I kept thinking, This is it. This is where my story ends.

All I wanted was for her to hold on. For both of us to survive.

I should've told the doctors and nurses what he did to me when they asked. What I was doing before contractions started. But, I protected him once more. He sat next to me in that hospital room, crying. All I could think to myself. "Why is he crying". "We're the ones who are hurt" When we returned to the resort, to finish the last few days of our vacation he cried. He apologized. He begged for forgiveness.

I had heard it all before.

By the time we returned home, I was numb. The fight had left me. I was living in survival mode, going through the motions, trying to make it to the next day.

Then, on December 21st, my water broke. On December 22nd, 1997, my daughter was born. She came into this world fighting. The umbilical cord was wrapped around her neck, and she struggled to breathe. She was taken to the ICU, tiny and fragile but alive.

I looked at her, and all I could think was how much she had already endured without even knowing it. I promised her that day that I would always protect her.

But promises made in moments of crisis are easy. Keeping them is the hard part.

When we left the hospital, I wanted to believe it was the start of something new. That maybe he would realize how close he had come to losing everything and finally change.

But the truth is, things didn't get better. They got worse.

The yelling didn't stop. The threats, the manipulation, the control—they were constant. And now, I wasn't just trying to protect myself. I was trying to protect two children.

It wasn't one incident, one moment, that pushed me to the edge. It was all of it—the slow unraveling, the endless cycle, the suffocating fear.

It was death by a thousand cuts.

The yelling. The accusations. The slammed doors.
The quiet manipulation that made me feel like I was the crazy one. The way he would break me down and then beg me to stay.

Every day felt like I was sinking, clawing for air while pretending I was fine.

And somewhere deep inside, a voice kept getting louder, whispering, "You can't survive this much

Until one night, I sat on the edge of our bed, staring at her crib, and realized I couldn't do it anymore.

I reached my breaking point.

And I knew, without a doubt, that something had to change.

Reflection

Chapter 2 was the unraveling.
And as I wrote those words, I could feel the weight of that time—the exhaustion, the fear, the confusion.

It's hard to explain what it's like to live in survival mode every day. To wake up wondering which version of the person you love will show up. To tiptoe around your own home, afraid of saying the wrong thing.

But the hardest part wasn't the violence—it was how deeply I began to believe I deserved it.

Looking back, I know now that I was never the problem.
The abuse wasn't love. It was control. And the unraveling wasn't the end—it was the start of something new, even if I couldn't see it yet.

If you are in that place right now, please know: You will make it out. There is life on the other side of the unraveling.

CHAPTER 3

The Journey Out

Some people think there's one clear moment when a person decides to leave. Like a light switch. A single incident. But the truth is, the decision happens slowly—one heartbreak, one betrayal, one bruise at a time—until something inside you snaps.

For me, it wasn't just one night. It was a collection of moments stacked on top of each other, pressing down on me until I couldn't breathe.

It was the nights I cried silently in the shower so my children wouldn't hear me. It was the mornings I plastered on a smile while feeling dead inside. It was the way I walked on eggshells in my own home, careful not to trigger another explosion. It was the constant, gnawing fear that one day, I wouldn't wake up at all.

But the night I realized I was completely lost came like a quiet storm.

One evening after another argument—one of hundreds—I found myself staring at my reflection in the bathroom mirror. My eyes were hollow. My face, unrecognizable. I didn't look like the woman I used to be. I looked like a ghost.

I placed my hands on the sink to steady myself, whispering under my breath, "How did I get here?"

That night wasn't loud. There were no slammed doors, no shouts, no bruises. Just silence. A heavy, suffocating silence that felt like death itself.

It was the weight of knowing I couldn't keep going like this.

In the weeks that followed, the control tightened even more. He started showing up unannounced at my job, asking questions that seemed harmless to outsiders but left me rattled. I'd catch him checking my phone, questioning who I was texting, accusing me of things I wasn't even thinking about. Asking myself, "Why did I let him get me a phone?"

The worst wasn't the yelling or the accusations—it was the quiet manipulations. The way he isolated me from people who cared. The way he made me doubt myself at every turn.

I remember one Sunday morning, I tried to leave the apartment to take my son to the park. He stood in front of the door, blocking my path, arms folded across his chest.

"Where do you think you're going?" he asked, voice low and dangerous.

"I just want to take him outside," I said quietly, my voice trembling despite how hard I tried to sound calm.

"Not without me."

It seemed so small. But it wasn't. It was control.
I could feel my son's eyes on me, watching how small I became in front of this man.

One afternoon, I stood in the kitchen, making dinner, when I felt the weight of it all hit me like a tidal wave. The sound of the stove, the kids' voices in the background, the TV playing —none of it could drown out the storm inside me.

I dropped the spoon in the sink and leaned against the counter, tears silently rolling down my face.

That's when I knew.

I wasn't living anymore—I was surviving.
And I couldn't survive like this much longer.

The final straw didn't come with violence. It came with indifference.

One night, after weeks of silent tension, I asked him—quietly, carefully—if we could talk. About us. About our family. About how things needed to change.

He didn't look up. He didn't even pretend to care.
That coldness cut deeper than any bruise ever had.

In that moment, I realized something terrifying. He wasn't going to stop. And if I didn't leave, one day, my children would be telling my story in past tense.

So I stopped waiting for the perfect moment to leave.
I stopped hoping he would change.

I started quietly gathering the broken pieces of my courage, stacking them like armor around my heart.

I didn't have all the answers yet.
I didn't have a plan.
But I had finally reached my breaking point.

And sometimes, that's all it takes to start saving yourself.

The Weight I Carried

I carried the weight of silence
like stones in my pocket,
each bruise, each broken promise
tucked deep where no one could see.

I wore smiles like armor,
laughed when I wanted to cry,
because falling apart
felt more dangerous than holding it in.

But even the heaviest burdens
can be set down.
Even the darkest night
gives way to morning.

And when I finally let go,
I learned to rise lighter
free and finally, whole.

CHAPTER 4

The Breaking Point

One night I sat on the edge of the bed, staring at my daughter's crib, something inside me cracked wide open. I had reached the edge of everything I thought I could endure. My body was exhausted. My spirit felt crushed. But looking at her peaceful, innocent face, I realized something crystal clear —I couldn't stay. Not anymore.

That night wasn't the first time I had thought about leaving— but it was the first time I truly meant it. I had spent years believing I could fix things, that if I stayed quiet, tried harder, loved better, he would finally become the man I wished he was.

But as I sat there in the darkness, listening to the sound of her soft breathing, I realized I had been fighting the wrong battle all along. It wasn't about saving him—it was about saving myself. Saving my children.

I knew it wasn't going to be easy. The fear wasn't just about him; it was about everything. Fear of what people would say. Fear of how I would survive financially. Fear of whether I was strong enough to do this alone. Fear of the fight that would come when he realized I was serious about leaving.

But there's a moment, a specific moment, when the pain of staying becomes far greater than the fear of leaving. That night, staring at her, that was my moment.

It wasn't just about me anymore. It was about the kind of life my daughter and my son were going to grow up in. I couldn't let them think that love was supposed to feel like walking on eggshells. I couldn't let them think that survival was the same thing as living.

I began to draft a plan quietly. I couldn't just leave recklessly. I had to be smart. I had to think of my children.

We had a joint bank account, where my paycheck was being deposited to. But, out of nowhere I started receiving child support for my oldest son. It was truly heaven sent. Every extra penny I could scrape together, I tucked away in a separate account he didn't know about. I stopped spending unnecessarily. I started preparing, little by little, chipping away at the trap he had built around me.

I also started gathering documents quietly—birth certificates, Social Security cards, important papers. It felt like preparing for war. Every time I moved something out of the apartment, packed a bag, or slipped cash into my hidden stash, my heart pounded in my chest like a drum. If he found out, I didn't know what would happen.

But the fear of staying had finally become heavier than the fear of leaving.

Eventually, I saved enough to start looking for an apartment. I did it in secret, scared every step of the way that he would find out. And when I finally got approved, I thought I had kept everything under wraps. But the landlord called the house to congratulate me, and he answered the phone.

The moment he told me about the call, my stomach dropped. I could feel the walls closing in, the weight of what I had been hiding crashing over me.

But instead of the explosion I expected, he was calm—too calm.

And that scared me even more. In some sick way, I think he enjoyed seeing me afraid. He acted like nothing was wrong, like he hadn't just uncovered the secret I had been desperately keeping. But that calm didn't last.

Later that evening, without warning, his rage surfaced like a storm. He shoved me so hard across the room that I lost my balance and tumbled down the steps. I can still remember the feeling—my body hitting each step, the sharp edges of fear and pain colliding, the sound of my own breath knocked out of me.

Lying at the bottom of those stairs, I realized that no amount of pretending could save me anymore. He wanted control—and if he couldn't keep it, he would break me trying.

Days passed, my bruises healed and he offered to help me move. I should have known better. I should have known that the calm was temporary—that he was already planning how to keep his hold on me.

But I took the help, desperate to avoid a fight.

He helped me pack. He loaded the car. He carried boxes into my new apartment like nothing was wrong.

For a moment, I believed maybe it really was over.

But the truth was, it was only the beginning of another battle.

Leaving isn't the end of the abuse—it's just the start of a new kind of fight. One that's quieter, but cuts just as deep.
A fight where the bruises no longer show, but the wounds still bleed beneath the surface. A fight against the echoes in your own mind, the nightmares that wake you in the middle of the night, the panic that grips your chest when the phone rings and it's a familiar number.

Freedom doesn't come with an apartment key or a court date. It's something you have to claw back piece by piece. Because even when you're physically free, your heart and mind are still untangling the chains he wrapped around you.

I learned quickly that freedom wasn't something you were handed—it was something you had to choose. Over and over again. Every single day.

You have to fight for it on the days when doubt creeps in. You have to fight for it when the guilt tries to convince you that maybe it wasn't that bad. You have to fight for it when your past tries to rewrite itself and tell you it was somehow your fault.

That's the battle no one talks about—the one after you leave.

But it's also where the healing begins.

One Thanksgiving, shortly after I moved, he offered to watch our daughter so I could go to my family's celebration. "Go enjoy yourself," he said. "I'll stay with her."

But there were always strings attached. Looking back now, I realize how often he used our daughter as a weapon. Every visit, every phone call, every gesture—it was all about control. He couldn't stand that I had walked away, so he found other ways to hold on.

That night, I came home and found the door chain locked from the inside. The bell I had hung on the doorknob was gone. I knocked, called his name—nothing. The lights were off, and the apartment was silent.

I remember standing in that hallway, heart racing, fists clenched, wondering how I had let it get this far.
Wondering how I was going to keep my children safe when every step forward felt like dragging the past behind me.

I had to call security to help me get inside. When they finally woke him up, they asked if he lived there. "No," he replied casually, "I'm just babysitting my daughter."

They told him to hand over the keys and leave. I knew he was boiling beneath the surface, but he complied. As he walked away, he asked, "Where am I supposed to go?"

I looked him straight in the eyes and said, "I don't care."
It wasn't the end, but it was the beginning of the end.

After that night, he ramped up his harassment. He would call my job repeatedly. He would call my home repeatedly. He's the reason til this day why I don't have a landline anymore.

Our visitation was horrible. No matter what, when he had visitation with our daughter, he'd find ways to make things difficult—keeping her school uniforms so I'd scramble to get replacements, returning her late, or demanding to change the schedule to suit his moods. He on two occasions didn't drop her off on the agreed date and that's when I had to get the police involved. I have never been so scared in my life.
I spend days thinking one day he would disappear with her and I would never see my daughter again.

It felt like I was living in two worlds. On the outside, I was working, taking care of my children, trying to rebuild a life.
On the inside, I was still trapped—always bracing for the next phone call, the next demand, the next reminder that I wasn't free yet. There were nights I would cry myself to sleep, wondering if I would ever feel peace again.

He then filed for custody, fabricating lies to make me look unstable and unfit. And just like that, I was thrust into the hardest fight of my life—a year-long custody battle that drained me financially, emotionally, and mentally.

It was exhausting, and terrifying. I had to hire an attorney. I had to endure invasive interviews from forensic psychologists. My family, my children, my home life—all picked apart and scrutinized.

But I fought. And when it was over, the court awarded me full custody.

But during that storm, something unexpected happened.
I met someone.

He wasn't supposed to be part of my story, not then, not in the middle of the chaos. But life has a way of surprising you. He came into my life quietly, without fanfare or grand gestures. And yet, he became the steady hand I didn't know I needed.

At first, I didn't trust it. I didn't know how to.
After everything I had survived, kindness felt foreign, almost suspicious. But little by little, he showed me that not everyone wanted to break me. That man would later become my husband.

From the very beginning, he saw me. Not just the broken pieces, not just the scared, exhausted woman fighting to survive—but all of me. He didn't judge me for my past or for the baggage I carried. He stood beside me when it would've been easier to walk away.

He could've easily walked away. Anyone would've understood if he said, "This is too much. I can't do this." But he didn't. He stayed. He supported me. He held my hand through every court date, every tear-filled night, every setback.

There were nights I would cry myself to sleep, the weight of everything crushing me, and he would quietly remind me, "You're not alone anymore."

When the court finally ruled in my favor, awarding me full custody of our daughter, I should have felt victorious. I should have celebrated. But all I felt was relief—and exhaustion. Because it wasn't just a legal battle I had survived. It was years of manipulation, control, and fear that I had finally started to break free from.

And I didn't do it alone.

For the first time in a long time, I wasn't fighting by myself.
Freedom wasn't a finish line—it was a journey.
And I was finally starting to believe that I deserved to walk it.

Beauty in The Broken

I was broken once,
scattered like pieces of shattered glass—
sharp edges, jagged memories,
wounds too deep for the naked eye to see.

I thought the cracks would define me,
that the scars would always whisper
of everything I had lost,
everything I would never be.
But life taught me something different.

That even broken things can shine.
That cracks let the light in.
That the pieces I thought made me weak
were the very things that made me whole.

I stitched myself back together,
not perfectly, not seamlessly,
but honestly—
with threads of grace, resilience, and love.

Now when I look at the woman in the mirror,
I don't see the damage.
I see the art. The masterpiece of survival.

And I hope you see it too—
in yourself, in your story,
in every scar and every tear you thought would break you.

You were never broken beyond repair.
You were always becoming
something beautiful.

CHAPTER 5

Rebuilding and Finding Love

Freedom doesn't come neatly packaged in a moment—it comes in layers, slowly peeling away the fear, the doubt, and the wounds you've been carrying for far too long.

No one tells you that the hardest part of leaving isn't the act of walking away—it's learning how to live again after you do. For so long, I had been living in survival mode. My days had been measured by how well I could avoid another explosion, how small I could make myself, how invisible I could become.

When the dust finally settled, I had to face the person I had become—and figure out how to rebuild her.

After the custody battle ended, life didn't magically get easier. There were still phone calls I didn't want to answer, still moments of anxiety when a familiar number appeared on my caller ID, still nights when the trauma replayed in my mind like an old, broken movie reel. The anxiety I felt whenever we had to be in the same space for our daughter.

But for the first time, I had space to breathe. I began to rebuild, brick by brick, piece by piece.

It wasn't easy. There were days I questioned if I had made the right decisions. Days I felt like I was barely holding it together, juggling motherhood, work, and the long, hard process of healing. I had spent so long in survival mode that I didn't even know what peace looked like.

I started by doing small things for myself. Playing music again. Dancing with my children in the living room. Singing at the top of my lungs while cooking dinner. Little by little, I stitched together the parts of me that I had buried.

And alongside all of that, there was someone who stood quietly beside me—the man I had met during the storm.
And slowly, I let him love me.

It wasn't easy at first. When you've spent years being told you're unlovable, it's hard to believe anyone could see you differently. When you've been taught that love is control, manipulation, and pain, it's hard to trust when someone shows you otherwise.

He had every reason to leave. What I came with wasn't easy. I had the scars of my past, the chaos of my present, and the uncertainty of my future. But he stayed. He stayed through the late-night phone calls from my abuser. He stayed through the long court hearings. He stayed when it became clear that being with me meant stepping into a world filled with complications.

But he showed me. He showed me that love didn't hurt.
That love didn't belittle. That love didn't demand you to shrink yourself. With him, I learned what it felt like to be safe. To be seen. To be loved without conditions or expectations.

It wasn't perfect. In fact, it was messy. I came with baggage, wounds that hadn't yet healed, a life in shambles. But he stayed. He didn't flinch when things got hard. He stood next to me when I was knee-deep in court papers, custody hearings, and fear. He didn't walk away when most people would've.

There were days when I tried to push him away, convinced I wasn't worthy of the love he offered so freely. But he never flinched. He never gave up. Even when I contemplated briefly going back to my ex. Yes, you read that right. It was my moment of insanity.

I had to straighten up really quick and realized I had fallen in love and I couldn't let that escape me. So, I fought for us and proved to him that there was no more room for my ex. So, I asked him to move in.

He reminded me, every single day, that I was more than what had happened to me. That I was worthy of peace.
That I deserved love without conditions.

But slowly, I began to rediscover who I was. I poured myself into my children. my bonus children. Their laughter, their needs, their growth—it all kept me moving forward. I focused on building a safe, loving home for them, one where they didn't have to tiptoe around anyone's anger or brace themselves for the next explosion. A place where they could just be kids.

And alongside all of that, there was someone who stood beside me—through it all.

We got married And our home became full—not just with children, but with laughter, warmth, and the kind of love that can only come after surviving something dark. Our children had a safe place to land, and I had a partner who stood beside me.

Life felt light again.

Another year passed and as life would have it. Along, came another surprise—a beautiful, unexpected gift. I became pregnant with my youngest son, A baby boy who completed our blended family in ways I didn't even know we needed. His arrival added another layer of joy to our home, another reason to keep moving forward, another light in a house that was once filled with shadows.

When I held him for the first time, I felt something I hadn't felt in years—hope. Pure, simple hope.

It reminded me how far I had come. How many nights I had cried, wondering if I would ever feel whole again. And there I was, holding a new life, knowing that the cycle had been broken.

There was so much love in our home during those years. The sounds of kids laughing, dancing, playing. Music playing in the background—always music, because that's how we lived. Sunday dinners, family gatherings, little moments that felt like everything I had fought for was finally falling into place.

But life isn't a straight line. After 15 years, my marriage ended too. For an entirely different set of reasons—reasons that are a story for another day, maybe even another book.

I won't get into the details here because this part of my journey wasn't about loss—it was about realizing that people come into our lives for a reason, sometimes for a season. That marriage wasn't a failure. It was a necessary chapter in my life. It taught me so much about love, about family, about myself.

And most importantly, it brought my bonus children into my life and gave me, my youngest son, who continues to fill my heart in ways no one else could.

Even after that chapter closed, I stood tall. Because by then, I knew who I was. I knew what I deserved. I knew that I could survive the unimaginable—and that I could thrive after it.

I had finally learned something that took me years to understand: That survival wasn't the end of the story. That healing was possible. That happiness wasn't something other people got to have—it was something I could create for myself.

And just when I least expected it, life showed me that love still had more to give me.

A quiet, steady, beautiful kind of love.

The kind I didn't have to fight for.
The kind that didn't hurt.
The kind that didn't come with conditions.

My now-husband and I had crossed paths long before we realized it. We were connected by people we both loved—his cousin has a child with one of my closest friend's sisters. We had been in the same rooms, the same family events, without knowing the role we would one day play in each other's lives.

My Soul Mate had arrived. My Best Friend.
It was simple, easy, natural.

He saw me—all of me.
The broken parts.
The strong parts.
The woman who had fought so hard to rebuild her life.

And he loved me anyway. During that time, love quietly entered my life again. It wasn't loud or dramatic. It was patient, gentle, and unexpected.

I met a man who finally saw all of me.

We talked for hours on the phone. What started as casual conversations quickly turned into something meaningful. We laughed. We talked about life, about my children, about everything in between. But more than anything, we talked about music.

That's where it all started—our connection over music.

I had always loved music. It was in my bones, a part of who I was. And as fate would have it, he was a part-time DJ. Unknowingly, we had this shared language, this way of communicating through lyrics, beats, and memories tied to every song. Music got me through my traumas and I believe it did the same thing for him.

Our conversations were endless. We would spend hours on the phone, talking about old-school jams, hip-hop, salsa, freestyle, R&B. The songs that shaped our childhoods, our heartbreaks, our victories. It felt like, through the music, we were slowly peeling back the layers of who we were.

And in those long conversations, we were vulnerable with each other

I shared parts of my past that I rarely spoke about. I told him about my father's battle with alcoholism, how it shaped me, how I lost him too soon. And he shared with me something that surprised me—that his own father, a man I would later come to adore, had once struggled with drug use.

That confession didn't push me away—it made me feel safe. It showed me that he knew what it was like to grow up watching someone you love fight demons they couldn't always control.

When I finally met his parents, I understood where he got his quiet strength from.

My father-in-law was the sweetest, humblest, most God-fearing man I have ever met. You would never know by looking at him that he had overcome so much. He greeted everyone with a smile, treated everyone like family, and carried himself with kindness and grace.

My mother-in-law became a light in my life. She is the most giving, loving, and spontaneous woman I've ever met—always going out of her way for me and my children, making us feel like we belonged. Her love wasn't performative; it was genuine, felt in every word, every gesture.

When my mother became sick, suffering two strokes and ending up in the hospital both times, it was my mother-in-law who stood beside me. She helped me feed my mom when I was too overwhelmed to do it alone. She supported me when the weight of everything felt unbearable. And when my mother passed away, she made sure I ate, made sure I was okay. She prayed for me. For us.

It wasn't just about the man I had met—it was about the family I was walking into. A family that felt like home in ways I never imagined.

He reminded me that I wasn't broken. That my story wasn't over. That I was worthy of the kind of love I once thought was only for other people.

Before we even said "I do," he and I took a leap of faith together. After 5 years of being together Instead of paying someone else's rent, we decided to buy our first home. It wasn't the "traditional" order of things. We hadn't lived together yet. We weren't married yet. But we trusted each other, trusted the life we were building.

Our house became a symbol of everything we had fought for —not just the physical structure, but the life, the love, and the peace that lived inside those walls.

It was the biggest blessing and when we felt the time was right we said I do and not one thing changed. We were still best friends and we have never allowed that to change.

Our marriage has never been about perfection. It's about partnership, respect, faith, and love—the kind that isn't loud or demanding, but steady and true

Now, nearly 13 years later, I can say without hesitation that this love saved me. Not because I needed someone to rescue me—I had already done that myself—but because I needed someone to remind me that love wasn't supposed to hurt.

And every single day, he continues to do just that.

The saying is true—you really do have to kiss a few frogs to find your prince.

I kissed more than my fair share.

But I wouldn't change my journey, because every piece of it brought me here. All of it—the pain, the struggle, the love, the loss—stitched me back together into someone stronger, wiser, and more whole than I ever thought I could be.

To love.
To freedom.
To peace.

And most importantly—to myself.

To My Younger Self
and My Children

Dear Jacqueline,

I see you. I see the hope in your eyes, the dreams in your heart, and the strength you don't even realize you have yet. You're standing at a crossroads, trying to find your way in a world that sometimes feels too heavy, too harsh, and too unkind. You're doing your best to survive, but I want you to know you're so much stronger than you think.

There will be moments when you feel lost, moments when the pain seems unbearable, and moments when you question your worth. But please, hold on. You are worth so much more than the words that cut you, the hands that hurt you, or the lies that try to define you. You will rise above it all.

I want to tell you something important: it's okay to ask for help. You don't have to carry the weight of the world on your shoulders. There are people who love you, people who want to support you, and people who will help you find your way out of the darkness. Don't be afraid to let them in.

One day, you will look back on these moments and realize that they didn't break you—they shaped you. You will find a strength inside yourself that you never knew existed, and you will use that strength to build a life filled with love, hope, and meaning.

And, most importantly, you will find peace. The journey won't be easy, but it will be worth it. Because one day, you will become the woman you were always meant to be.

With love and pride,
Jacqueline

My Dearest Princess

From the moment I held you in my arms, I knew you were special. You were so tiny, so perfect, and yet so strong. You came into this world fighting, and you've been a fighter ever since.

You may not realize it, but you saved my life. There was a moment, years ago, when I felt so broken, so lost, that I didn't know if I could go on. But then I looked at you, lying peacefully in your crib, and everything became clear. I couldn't leave. I couldn't let him win. And I couldn't let you grow up in a world where he had all the power.

You gave me a reason to fight when I didn't have the strength to fight for myself. You reminded me of what love truly is— unconditional, unwavering, and boundless. You were my light in the darkest moments, my hope when everything felt hopeless.

As you've grown, I've watched you face challenges that no child should have to endure. I've seen your pain, your struggles, and your tears. But I've also seen your strength, your resilience, and your ability to rise above it all. You are a miracle, Mima. You are my miracle.

I want you to know how proud I am of you. You have taught me more about love and courage than I ever thought possible. And no matter what life throws your way, I will always be here for you, cheering you on, holding your hand, and reminding you of just how incredible you are.

Thank you for being my light, my joy, and my reason for everything. I love you more than words could ever express.

Forever and Always
Mom

Dear Billy, Pablo, Tevan, Justin, Mariah, and Ryan,

You are each a part of my heart, and every day I am grateful for the joy, love, and purpose you brought and continue to bring into my life. Being your mother has been my greatest honor, and I want you to know how deeply I love you—all of you, each in your own unique way.

Justin, my firstborn, you taught me what it meant to love unconditionally. From the moment I held you in my arms, I realized my heart was no longer just my own. You gave me strength and purpose, even when life was at its hardest. Watching you grow into the person you are today fills me with so much pride.

Billy and Pablo, you came into my life and taught me what it means to embrace love in all its forms. You didn't just join the family; you became a part of my heart.

Tevan, my son you've always shown me kindness from the day we met and shared my love of scary movies by holding on tight to me. You have shown me the importance of finding joy, even in the smallest moments by watching what an amazing husband and father you've become.

My Mariah, my beautiful daughter you have brought light and laughter into my life. From the beginning, you've held a special place in my heart. Your kindness, strength, and determination inspire me every day. Watching you and the amazing woman and mother you have become has been beyond my imagination. My heart is full

My Pop-pop, my youngest, my baby, you are the reminder that even in life's most unexpected moments, beauty and love can grow. Your energy and spirit keep me going, and you've shown me that the future holds so much promise.

Each of you has shaped me in ways I can never fully express. Through the ups and downs, you have been my anchors, my reason for continuing to fight, and my hope for the future. I know I wasn't always perfect, and I know our lives weren't always easy, but please know this: everything I did, and everything I do is for you.

I hope you see in yourselves what I see in you—a strength that can weather any storm, a heart big enough to love unconditionally, and a spirit that can light up the darkest days. You are my greatest accomplishments, and I am so proud of who you are and the people you are becoming.

Thank you for loving me, for forgiving me, and for being the incredible individuals that you are and for promoting me to grandma, and wela. I love you all more than words can ever say.

Lastly, To My Grandchildren. I thought there could not be a bigger love than loving your Mommy and Daddy. Boy, was I wrong. You are the very best of them with the cherry on top. I love you.

With all my heart,
Mommy, Mom, Mother, Madre, Mother Dearest
(IYKYK),Grandma, Wela & Jackie

Dear Beautiful Soul,

If you're reading this and you're still in the middle of your storm, I want you to hear me clearly:

You are not crazy.
You are not weak.
You are not alone.

The pain you're feeling right now—the fear, the confusion, the exhaustion—it's real. But it's not the end of your story.

There will be a day when the chains fall off, when the fear fades, when you breathe deeply again. It might not feel possible right now, but I promise you—freedom is waiting for you.

You don't have to have it all figured out.
You just have to take one step.
And then another.
And then another.

You are worthy of a life without fear.
You are worthy of love that doesn't hurt.
You are worthy of peace.

And when you're ready to walk away, I'll be here, on the other side of the storm, waiting to welcome you home.

With love and hope,
Jacqueline

MOMENTS OF

Gratitude

Gratitude has been my anchor through life's storms. Even in the darkest moments, there were glimmers of light—acts of kindness, moments of faith, and reminders that I was not alone. These are the moments that helped me hold on, even when I felt like letting go.

My faith has always been my guiding light. In the moments when I felt completely lost, I turned to prayer. I prayed for strength when I felt weak, for hope when the future seemed hopeless, and for protection when fear consumed me. Faith was the thread that held me together, even when everything else seemed to unravel.

There were times when I felt like God had forgotten me, but looking back now, I can see His hand in so many parts of my life. The courage to leave, the strength to start over, the people who entered my life at just the right time—all of it was part of a greater plan. My faith reminded me that even when I couldn't see the path ahead, I could trust that I was being led somewhere better.

Unexpected Kindness

I'll never forget the acts of kindness that came from the most unexpected places.

A neighbor who smiled and held the elevator door when I was barely holding it together inside.

A coworker who noticed I hadn't eaten all day and quietly left lunch on my desk without asking questions.

A stranger in a waiting room who complimented me on my children, reminding me, without knowing, that I was doing something right.

These small gestures may have seemed insignificant to the people who offered them, but to me, they were lifelines.

There was a day I'll never forget.

I was overwhelmed by bills, unsure of how I would keep everything together. I hadn't told anyone how much I was struggling—I was too ashamed.

One afternoon, a friend handed me an envelope without saying a word. Inside was enough money to pay a bill I had been dreading. It wasn't just about the money—it was the reminder that someone saw me, that I wasn't invisible.

Another moment that still sits in my heart was when my son's teacher reached out to me after noticing how withdrawn he had become. She didn't know what was happening in our home, but her compassion and quiet attention to my son reminded me that there were good people in the world, looking out for us, even when we didn't ask.

The Strength of Community

My family and close friends became my support system when I needed it most. Even when I was hesitant to share what I was going through, they stood by me, ready to lift me up. My closest friend, in particular, was a constant source of encouragement. She reminded me of my worth when I forgot it myself and gave me the space to heal in my own time.

There were phone calls when I just needed to cry. Late-night conversations that turned into therapy sessions. Text messages that simply said, "I'm thinking of you."

These small moments added up to something bigger—proof that I wasn't alone.

It wasn't just the people I knew—it was the broader community as well. The resources and organizations I discovered gave me hope that I wasn't alone in my struggle. Knowing that others had walked this path before me and found a way out reminded me that I could, too.

There were also unexpected kindnesses from strangers in waiting rooms, from nurses who took extra time with me when I was at my lowest, from a woman at the laundromat who offered to watch my kids for a moment when I looked like I was falling apart.

These may seem like small things to some, but when you're surviving trauma, these tiny gestures are everything.

A Grateful Heart

Looking back, I am filled with gratitude—not just for the good moments, but for the hard ones, too. Every challenge taught me something about myself, about resilience, and about the power of hope. I am grateful for the strength I didn't know I had, for the people who stood by me, and for the faith that carried me through.

I am grateful for my children, who gave me a reason to keep going. For my family and friends, who never stopped believing in me. For the strangers whose small acts of kindness made all the difference. For the readers of this book, who will carry this story forward and use it to build hope in their own lives or for someone they love.

These moments of gratitude are what keep me grounded. They remind me that even in the most difficult times, there is always something to be thankful for.

And they inspire me to pay it forward, to be a source of light and kindness for others who may be walking their own difficult path.

and Finding Freedom

Escaping abuse and rebuilding your life is one of the hardest journeys you'll ever take, but it's also one of the most courageous. I know how overwhelming it can feel—how the fear, shame, and uncertainty can paralyze you. But I want you to know that you are not alone, and there are steps you can take to regain your power and move toward safety.

I also want you to understand that healing is not linear. Some days you'll feel strong. Some days you'll feel like you're back at square one. That's normal. What matters is that you keep going.

Here are some of the steps I took—and the ones I wish I had taken sooner:

1. Trust Your Instincts

If something feels wrong, trust that feeling. Abuse often starts subtly, with words or actions that may seem insignificant at first. Pay attention to those moments and listen to the voice inside you that says, "This isn't okay."

You don't need proof to leave. You don't need anyone else's permission. If you feel unsafe, that is reason enough.

2. Document Everything

Keep a record of incidents, no matter how small they seem. Write down dates, times, and details of abusive behavior. Take pictures of injuries if it's safe to do so. Save threatening messages or emails.

This can be helpful if you need to pursue legal action, seek a restraining order, or file for custody later on.

I didn't know the importance of documentation back then—but I wish I had. It can protect you later when your story is being questioned.

3. Build a Support Network

This is not a journey you should take alone.

Reach out to trusted friends, family members, or coworkers. Let someone know what's happening, even if it feels uncomfortable. You don't have to disclose everything at once— but let at least one person know what's really going on.

If you don't feel safe talking to someone you know, connect with a local domestic violence advocate or counselor. There are people trained to help you.

4. Create a Safety Plan

One of the hardest things about leaving is figuring out how to do it safely. Here are some steps you can take:

- Identify a safe place you can go if you need to leave quickly.
- Memorize or save important phone numbers (friends, family, hotlines) in case you lose access to your phone.
- Pack a bag with essentials and keep it in a safe, hidden place:
- IDs and important documents
- Keys
- Cash or debit card
- Medications
- A change of clothes for you and your children
- Any copies of restraining orders or legal documents

Your safety plan is your lifeline. Even if you're not ready to leave today, having a plan will make the difference when the moment comes.

5. Seek Professional Help

You don't have to carry this burden alone.

Therapists, counselors, and support groups can provide a safe space to process your emotions and begin healing. If you have children, find resources that can support them too. The trauma touches them, even when you try to shield them from it.

Healing is possible—but you need support.

6. Use Available Resources

There are organizations dedicated to helping victims of domestic violence. These organizations can provide shelter, legal assistance, counseling, and more. You deserve support, protection, and a path to freedom.

For Victims of Abuse

Domestic Violence Hotlines and Organizations
• National Domestic Violence Hotline (U.S.): 1-800-799-7233 or text START to 88788
www.thehotline.org
Provides 24/7 confidential support, resources, and safety planning.
• Love Is Respect: 1-866-331-9474
Offers support for young people in abusive relationships.

Counseling and Support Groups
• RAINN (Rape, Abuse & Incest National Network): 1-800-656-HOPE
www.rainn.org
Offers resources for survivors of sexual violence.
• Search for local support groups that provide community and healing.

Local Shelters and Legal Aid
• Contact local domestic violence shelters in your area.
• Many offer emergency shelter, counseling, case management, and legal assistance.
• Legal Aid organizations may offer free or low-cost representation for restraining orders, custody, and divorce.

Online and Community Support
• Search for local support groups or online survivor forums.
• Many organizations offer virtual support groups, trauma-informed therapy, and survivor resources.

For Immigrant or Undocumented Survivors
• Many domestic violence organizations provide confidential support, regardless of immigration status.
• National Immigrant Women's Advocacy Project: www.niwap.org

For Male Survivors
• The Domestic Abuse Helpline for Men and Women: Call 1-888-743-5754

For LGBTQ+ Survivors
• The Anti-Violence Project:
Call 1-212-714-1141
Website: www.avp.org

Starter Kit

I want to leave you with more than just my story.
Here are a few things that helped me along the way—things I hope will help you, too.

Journal Prompts:
• What does safety mean to me?
• What are three things I love about myself?
• When was the last time I felt free?
• What would I say to my past self if I could?

Self-Care Checklist:
• Take a walk outside
• Play your favorite song and dance without caring who's watching
• Write yourself a love letter
• Call a friend who makes you laugh
• Rest without guilt

Books & Podcasts I Recommend:
• The Body Keeps the Score by Bessel van der Kolk
• Untamed by Glennon Doyle
• We Can Do Hard Things Podcast
• Permission to Heal Podcast

Remember: Healing isn't selfish—it's necessary.

Remember, You Deserve Safety and Freedom

Leaving an abusive situation is never easy, but it is possible. You deserve a life free from fear, filled with love and dignity.

Every step you take, no matter how small, is a victory. And even if it feels impossible right now, there is hope. You are not defined by what you've been through—you are defined by the strength it takes to rise.

Stitching the Pieces Together

As I reflect on my journey, I see a tapestry of experiences—some beautiful, some painful, all of them essential to the person I've become. My life hasn't been perfect, but it's been mine. Each thread of joy, heartbreak, resilience, and love has come together to create something whole.

For years, I believed that my story was something I had to survive in silence. That the scars I carried—both visible and invisible—were something to hide. But today, I understand that my story is my power.

My legacy isn't just about what I've endured—it's about what I've overcome. It's about the lessons I've learned and the love I've shared. It's about the family I built, the children I raised, and the person I fought to become.

I want my children to know that they are the brightest lights in my life, the reason I kept fighting when it felt like I had no more fight left. They are my heart, and they carry my hopes for the future. But I also want every reader of this book to know that your story matters, too.

I hope you see in these pages that survival is not the end—it's the beginning. That healing is possible. That you are not defined by what was done to you, but by how you rise afterward.

I spent years stitching my broken pieces back together. And now, I can look at those seams—the places where I was torn apart and then mended—and see something beautiful.

This realization led me to work as a Social Work Assistant. This role allows me to provide immediate support and resources to individuals in need of mental health services. Engaging in this work enables me to stand alongside individuals during some of their most vulnerable moments, offering empathy, understanding, and resources to aid in their recovery.

In addition it also let me become certified in disaster response crisis counseling. This specialized training equips me to assist communities and individuals affected by disasters, providing psychological first aid and emotional support in times of crisis. By stepping into this role, I aim to contribute to the resilience and recovery of those impacted by unforeseen tragedies.

These pursuits are more than professional endeavors; they are deeply personal missions. Whilst the disaster response crisis counselor is a volunteer role. This experience empowers me in helping others, I find purpose and fulfillment, transforming past pain into a source of strength and support for those in need.

That is my legacy.

Be The Light

This isn't just my story—it's a call to action for all of us to be the light in someone else's darkness.

If you know someone who is struggling, reach out. Offer a kind word, a listening ear, or a helping hand. You may not be able to fix everything, but sometimes, knowing someone cares is enough to give someone the courage to keep going.

If you've experienced abuse or trauma yourself, I want you to hear me clearly:

You are not broken. You are not alone. You are not defined by your pain.

You have the power to heal. To rebuild. To thrive.

Your voice has power. Your story can inspire others to find their strength. Your healing can become a roadmap for someone who doesn't believe freedom is possible.

For those in positions of power—leaders, educators, advocates —use your platform to raise awareness about domestic violence and abuse. Advocate for better resources, stronger protections, and more support for survivors.

Together, we can create a world where every person has the opportunity to live free from fear and harm.

How You Can Help

If reading my story has moved you, here are ways you can take action:

• Donate to local shelters and victim advocacy organizations.
• Volunteer your time, whether it's answering hotline calls, mentoring survivors, or organizing community events.
• Share resources with someone who may need them—you never know who's quietly struggling.
• Use your voice to speak out against abuse in your community.
• Be a safe person. Sometimes, all someone needs is one person who believes them, who listens without judgment, who helps them take the first step toward freedom.

And finally, to the readers who are walking through their own storms, I want you to remember this:

You are not defined by what has happened to you. You are defined by the strength it takes to keep going. There is life after trauma, and there is hope on the other side of the pain.

You are not alone. Whether you've walked a similar path, know someone who has, or simply needed to hear this story to understand the strength of survival—you are now part of this journey.

Life will continue to test you. There will be days when the weight of your past feels heavier than usual. But I hope you carry these pages as a reminder that even after the darkest night, the sun still rises.

You are capable of rebuilding. You are worthy of peace. You are worthy of love—the kind that doesn't hurt, the kind that feels safe.

If my story has shown you anything, let it be this: You can fall apart, stitch yourself back together, and become something even stronger and more beautiful than you were before.

Your story isn't over. It's only just beginning.

Be the light—for yourself, for others, and for the world around you. Together, we can create something beautiful out of the broken pieces.

Stitched Together With Good Intentions

www.ingramcontent.com/pod-product-compliance
Lightning Source LLC
Chambersburg PA
CBHW071541120626
46550CB00006B/2540